This page is intentionaly left blank.

"MY WORDS...

Shanel Morae

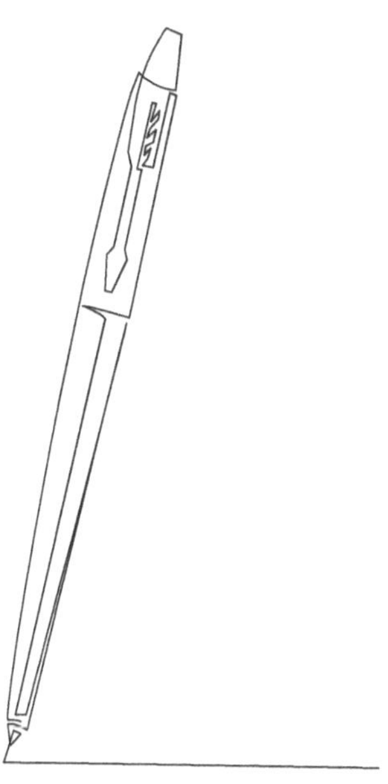

The Feathered Traveler

“My Words...

Shanel Morae

Published by:
Feathered Traveler

Typesetting: Bre’ana Nash

Cover Design & Illustrations: Bre’ana Nash

A CIP record for this book is available from the Library of Congress Cataloging-in-Publication Data

ISBN-13: 979 8 59267 132 6

Printed in USA

Dedicated to

"To my mother and father, John Matthews and Regina B. Scott. Thank you for giving the greatest parts of you to me. I know you are proudly watching over me. I love and miss you each and every day. Rest in paradise, my warrior and my queen."

"PREFACE...

The thing about life is that it is forever changing and constantly throwing curve balls in every path we take, but we have a choice in how we react to those spins.

In my 30 years of life, I've had many curve balls thrown in my path and each time I was faced with the decision to either let it take me down or rise above. There were times when giving up was presented and I embraced it wholeheartedly. It didn't feel good and neither did the circumstances that crossed my path; lying down was easy. Other times I chose to overcome my battles and fight for my sanity, my peace, my love; I was fighting for me.

Confronting my struggles was the best option and that's when I realized that I never gave up. I learned that rest is what I needed to recalibrate and reevaluate my life. My biggest struggle is dealing with the loss of others and myself. I lost both of my parents when their guidance was needed the most. The struggle to truly find myself was the most daunting task I've ever had to endure and while I could have completely given up, I chose to heal.

Not just from the loss of my family but from the wounds of life's extra curve balls. I knew that I needed to heal myself in order to handle what came next. In doing so, the universe showed me that with the bad comes the incredible: abundance, light, love... Wholeness.

After their passing, I walked into my purpose with more meaning. It was not and is not an easy task, but it is definitely worth all the work I've put into it. I am introduced to new experiences that are life-altering and I am seeing beauty surround me. I have reconnected with myself and found that I am in a place where all my dreams are coming true. I still have work to do everyday when it comes to restoring myself, but I've become addicted to the healing process. I am in love with life and everything attached.

This book is an expression of my pain, my growth, and my love. "My Words... is about the process of changing, growing and loving every moment of it. My hope is that you will have the courage to face yourself. That you become inspired to join me on this journey of healing and loving yourself more and more everyday. I wish peace and blessings on all of you and I hope you take something away from these words and treat them as your own. My heart is my gift to you. Take care and enjoy.

Just in case no one has told you today and forever,

I love you!

Shanel Morae

"CONTENTS...

"INTRODUCTION...

There are nights I lie awake thinking about every scenario from the start of my life to present day occurrences. Some nights my spirit is low and all the worst moments I've had drive donuts around my thoughts. Other nights my energy is high and my wanderlust sets in on some of the best feelings. While that sounds like a drift I love to be on, my point of this is... I lie awake.

I've been awake for most of my life. Of course I sleep, but on the nights I couldn't and can't, words would dance around in my head and form stories I thought people only dreamed about. These words describe my innermost thoughts and feelings in a sentence flow that is far from simple subject and predicate etiquette. On those very nights I'd take out my notebook and allow my pen to run out of ink. Lyrical patterns and rhyme schemes cried out the way I couldn't. After writing them, my spirit was less burdened and rest became my friend. These words were there to understand me, and find out who I was. These words were there to teach me lessons, to hurt me, to love me... They were there to guide and show me where I've been and where I'm going. My words have been there to get me through life's changes and they've helped me sleep many nights. The most important lesson I've learned is that these words loved me and were... me.

For all these reasons, I love these words, or should I say my words...

"In my words

I find new love
A lasting love
A true love

In my words...

My pages are honest
My pages are flawed
My pages shed tears
My pages share love
My pages make love

In my words...

My pages scream

FUCK!

My pages are vulnerable
My pages are expressive
My pages are changing...

...but most importantly,

My pages are mine...

"I'M TERRIFIED OF

CHANGE

BUT...

THE REAPER'S BEAUTIFUL COLLECTION

"I saw my life pass before
their eyes
I heard cries that no longer
made sounds
Pain that was no longer felt
Sadness that sank into the mud created
by my rain...

They left me,
everything from the beginning changed
My life started over as theirs ended
My thoughts knew no boundaries,
no sense of time,
no coming,
just going...

The Reaper's beautiful collections

Life changed,
On my own
Feeling alone,
No eyes to look into and find my soul
Only me...
Who will answer these questions?
Make these phone calls?
Embrace my hugs?
Have my back?

Say "I love you" back??
Life changed...

Wings
So beautiful
At one point I wanted some
To join in the change they
involuntarily made
Except mine
Mine would have been my sacrifice
I wanted to be in the collection
But...

I was given feathers...
I saw a different light,
That turned dark nights
into bright thoughts
That made rainy days feel like love
That made the clouds feel like
protection...

Soon, I accepted the change,
I've never seen so many beautiful days
It's as if they know
I'm looking for them
and they paint my favorite hues
in the sky

I can't choose between
sunset or sunrise
So both if it was painted by them...
They left me
but...

They watch over me...

BEAUTY BECOMES ME

Once I read a poem by Andrea Gibson
The famous words, "It hurts to become"
I realized that there was truth in it
There was a life waiting to emerge
But this is not roses
Candy not included
Some walks in the park
That come with trips and falls
It's turbulent waters
Unfinished construction work
Potholes in roads that need to be filled
It's tears your eyes were afraid to shed
But
There is more laughter
More smiles
And an abundance of love

It's the shedding of what I thought I was...
And became who I truly am...
When I accepted change,
Change became me....
And let me tell you, my dear
IT. IS. BEAUTIFUL!

BEAUTIFULLY FLAWED SYSTEM

"I am programmed
And yet flawed
A faulty system
I am not a human being
Just simply an abomination
To the highest being
Created for a mission
Code: Save Me

Take me from this hellhole
Decorated with restraints
shackles and bondages
But wait...
Is that not what I like?
Pain and suffering
Frantic thoughts
Captivity of the mind
Because after all, we as "human beings"
Are kinky like that
Constant obsessions with negativity
Continuous bonds with the acts of
distress
Repeated confrontations with self
A lack of respect for ourselves
Themselves, yourself, myself... self

But!
I am not a human being
Just simply an abomination
To the highest being
Created for a mission
Code: Rescue Me

Redeem the life
That ran out of existence
According to the womb that bared me
Who am I?
A simple program
Given life to play a game
Placed on a field
Where you and I play these
hunger games...
The highest being
Watching from the skybox
Is this to make sure we have
a guaranteed seat?
I wait patiently for my command...

I am knocking on the door of life
But I could have sworn
I was already welcomed in
Maybe...
I am a faulty system

Flawed
Riddled with viruses
Troubleshooting questions from my
central processing units,
A program in need of debugging
There's a tick... tick... ticking
in this corner
And a wire hanging in the other
For I am not like the others
Divergent in manner
Eccentric in character
Perhaps I am the upgrade
Code: Fix me

Maybe I am NOT the abomination
Just simply an enhancement
Made to lead missions
Code: Save them
A new system for lasting durability
A guaranteed transmission
Avant-garde of models
I am the special encryption...
Code: Restore Them"

TEARS OF JOY

"I want a joy
that rains
Buckets full
Canisters refilled
My well runneth over

I want a joy
that pours
Fill my cup
Overquench my thirst
Spill through threads
Stitched for shelter

I want a joy
that floods
Ravish through dark alleys
Wash away walls built by stones
Irrigate dreams planted in dry soil

I want a joy
that rains
In abundance
Replenish me
And swallow me whole...

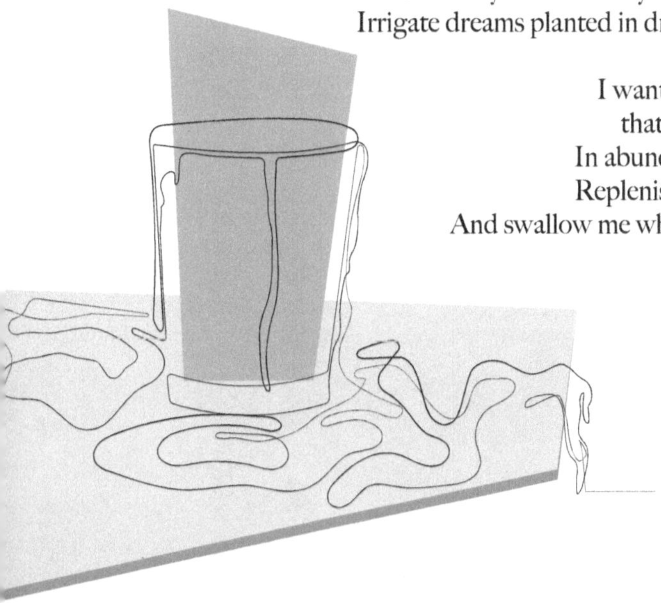

REOCCURENCE

"Everyday I wake up
I swear my dream world is still
going...
Fairytales and fantasies
Linger on the sand dust of my eyelashes
An extra dose of possibilities

My dreams share worlds that collide
in time
My dreams share worlds that love to
rhyme

I sleep in blissful slumber
Wake up to thoughts that wonder
Somewhere I've never been
And yet I'm already there...
I'm here...
Everyday
Every night
Is this what reoccurrence feels like?"

OLD TO ME, NEW TO YOU

"I have a habit of
reverting back to old ways
Old flames
Old names

Growth taught me...
Brought me
New waves
New perspectives
A new flame
And rid me of shame

I've found it hard
to let old things die
But on a balance scale
My presence outweighs my past
I've learned to focus on new views
My world is filled with new truths
New moves
And in that I find myself renewed

Today I sing to the tunes of new songs
Write with the ink of new woes
Spill lines that create new poems

Had it not been for the past tense

My old sense
My present day wouldn't know such freedom
I'm grateful for new peace
New reasons to believe
New opportunities to receive

Now I refer to old ways
Showing gratitude while focusing on new days"

TRANSMUTATION

"There were days I looked up at the sky
and said
"Today you look different"
Some days the sky had marks in places
it was touched
Showing me I, too, have scars in
beautiful territories
by placeholders
not meant to be kept
by ideas
that didn't belong in my thoughts
Other days the sky filled with clouds
Teaching me that light would always
be there but
Maybe somedays I wouldn't see the
outcome
But I'd be reminded that it was just
behind the noise
There were days the sky was rainy and
murky
Telling me it's okay to be
overwhelmed with emotions
Tears were needed
to cleanse my grounds
And water the seeds I've planted
Then...
There was the sun

and transparent skies
Affirming that despite all of the
changes
Radiant days are always on the rise...
Through it all I'll still have my shine"

'NIGHT SKIES
GET THE BEST
OF ME...

INVISIBLE

"It's distant, clammy, & drenched
Moods affect moods
Troubles affect walls that stumble
Slip, trip, & fall

Eyes close
Eyes open
Eyes close
As the color of stone cold takes over
Breathing in hallow winds
Blowing out cold fronts
Winds so hard
Knock me down
Slip, trip, & fall
Moods affect moods
Blending into the darkness
Screaming,
"CAN YOU HEAR ME?"
......
"CAN YOU SEE ME?"
......
Feed into the life
Lying on the ground
Gasping for air
Choked by the smoke
Of the midnight car that drove by
"WAIT!"

……

Forgotten

Fading in the background
Trench coat
Sabled beanie
Black boots
Black...
Eyes close, eyes open
No colors
Just black

Slip, trip, & fall
On black clouds
Dull stars
Dry planet
My dimly lit universe

It's distant, clammy, & drenched
Moods affect moods
Eyes open, eyes close
Eyes close

I slipped
I tripped
I fell
Into a blended darkness..."

AT NIGHT, WE BATTLE...

They say rest is the best thing for you
How am I supposed to sleep when my
thoughts are awake?
Where do my obscene scenarios end?
When do my peaceful dreams begin?

Questions
Thoughts
Visions
Worries
Doubts

Idle chatter becomes me
whisper
'Close your eyes...

...inhale...

...exhale...

There... is your peace
Now sleep, my love

Rest conquers me...

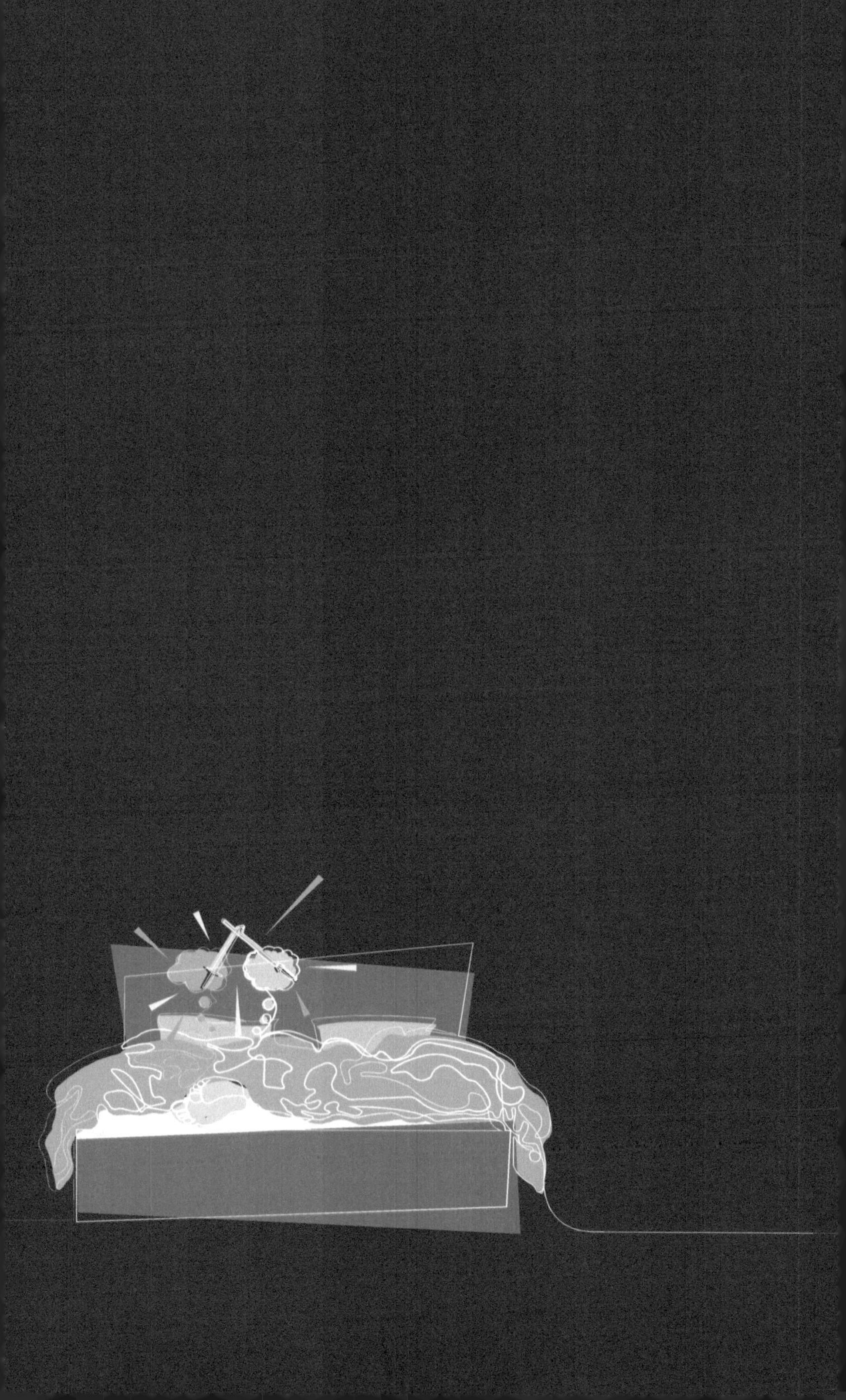

YESTERDAY

"I used to worry about yesterday
I worried about today
Every night
I worry about tomorrow
I would lie awake checking the weather
for tomorrow
Just to see what my mood would feel
like
I checked my horoscope from the day
before
Just to see if my yesterday would affect
my today...

But today...
Today I tried to worry about yesterday
And it told me,
"'No matter what happened yesterday
Today, you woke with hope and a
smile
Because you made it
And the weather feels like life
And your horoscope is filled with
infinite possibilities
So tonight, instead of worrying, be
reassured
Be encouraged...
be...

HUNTING FOR SERENITY

"When my thoughts run into the wild
I remember this:
Even the jungle calms down;
Sit in silence
The woods speak words unsaid;
Listen to your heart
Nature needs exploration;
Get lost in that moment
The forest provides shelter in itself;
Rest in you...

There I find new possibilities
New roots from the seeds I've planted
New ground I've covered
There
I find me"

LEAD ME TO RELEASE

"At night I cried tears only she knew
about
I said words only she would listen to
She stopped me mid scream,
'The worry isn't yours
The stress isn't yours
The heartbreak IS yours
But only for a little while...

Let them go

Allow yourself to mourn,
Grieve the relationship,
Bemoan the failures,
Lament what was lost,
Then

Let them go'"

-a text from my sister

LEVITATION

"Lift me
When my spirits are down
Fill my storm clouds
With pleasantly scented thoughts
Take me to a zone
That reaches altitudes untouched
By the likeness of apathy

Elevate me
In my gracious hours
When the trumpet sounds
And the light sparks
Celebrate me
Until I feel like your highness

Stimulate me
Take me to a place
Where my soul intertwines with
another
And we float with the same
nebulas
We created in both roll up sessions
...if you catch my drift...

Transcend me
Til I'm my most authentic being
Help me surpass levels

Far beyond my eyes can see

By now I've reached my zenith
Here, my cerebral defies gravity
My state is climactic
I. Am. Divine."

CARES OF MY WORLD

"And when night falls
I rest my mind on you
Your head next to mine
In that I find peace
When night terrors arise
You lock your hand in mine
And without notice
You become my release...
When I wake up to hear
The world has burned
I smile
because well...
My world is next to me
With a smile as bright as the fire in the
forests
With you I can
take off my mask
Because the only contagion I want to
catch is your passion
And when the missiles hit;
Because they will
I'll know you launched them in
climactic exchanges
You see,
I can't be bothered with the worries
and cares of the world
Because when night falls

I rest my mind on you
Your head next to mine
Rest assured,
I find peace with us...

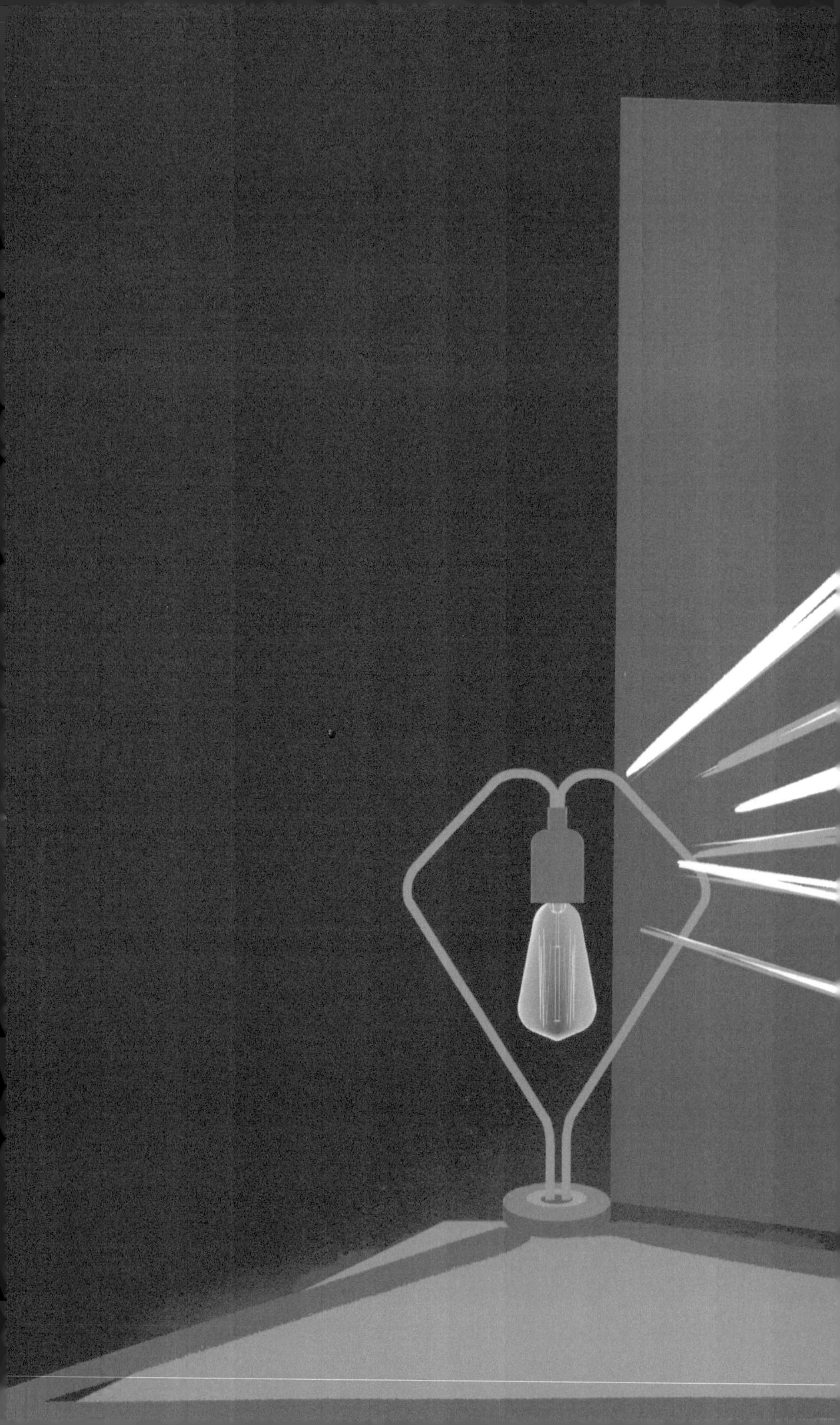

"LET LOVE
BE MY
LAMP...

"TO: ME

Show me love
I've never felt before
Bring me joy
That leaps beyond mountain views
Release endorphins
Suppressed by outside intensities
That made me feel as if contentment
was as far as I could reach...

I often heard of such affections
I saw this glowing warmth surround
others
And instantly my pursuit grew stronger
From one being to the next substance
I came up short
Of course
I gave up
And then it happened...

I met you
Someone familiar
So kind and gentle
You knew me

Felt me
Embraced me
And everyday I focused on getting to
know you
I realized you chose me...
always and forever
Everything I was searching for rested
in you

Affection
Warmth
Happiness
Wholeness
Love
You gave me all and more

I'm so glad I found you
More importantly,
I'm so lucky you never left

Signed,
Me"

GRACIOUS GRATITUDE

"Just in case
Nobody's told you
I place my gratitude in you
Each day you wake me up
A luminescent smile
That lifts me up
I'm captivated in your incandescent
love

I value the vistas from you
The night and morning dew from you
The sky holds many hues of you
I want you to know,
I appreciate you

Just in case
Nobody's told you
I place my love in you"

SIGHTSEEING

"My nightly visions
Get tangled in your daily views
Oh, how I love to look at you...
I once thought dreams only existed
When your eyes were closed but
I pinched myself and you were still
here...

I opened my eyes
And there you were sound asleep
Tucked away in my solicitude
Safe and secure...

And if this is a dream
I pray everyday
To stay in this wonderland
Together, we are touched by divinity
Blessed by God...
My prayers were answered;
I'm lost in true virtue

Sheesh...
I swear I love you"

WHERE IT GOES I WILL FOLLOW

"They say
Following your heart
will lead you astray
But...
For every moment
I've followed my heart
I was lifted by the highs of pheromones
And beautifully fragrant mist
Eyes sparkled brighter than fresh dew
on morning flowers
I was captivated in the pleasures of
word play
Reassurance consumed my thoughts
Countless acts of service were found
along the path

For every moment
I've followed my heart
My thoughts were renewed
I found new passions
Creativity became my existence
Invincibility was my vice

My heart has led me to the art of
shattered pieces
Different worlds of convoluted
thoughts

Thunderstorms outnumbered by tears
Personas unrecognizable by my
reflection
And even in that,
I wouldn't say astray

Following my heart gave me presence
Experience was the true gift
Potential was in reach

Following my heart led me to...
'Me

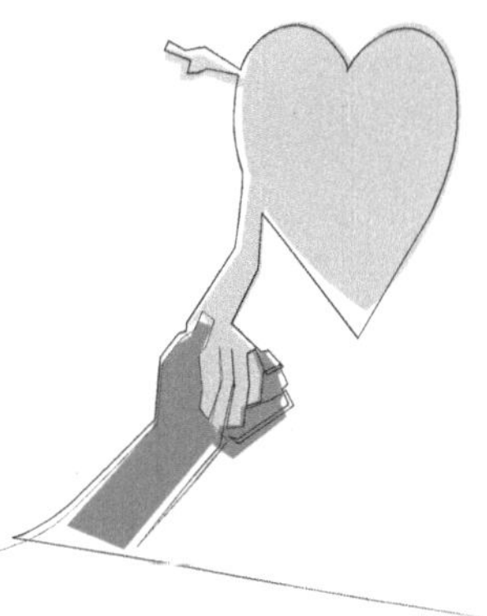

FREEDOM

"I, once, saw a feather
Float onto the helm of my jacket
Soft and gentle
Drifting freely
I thought
'What an honor
To be chosen by
this type of love
The wind could have taken you
anywhere
Instead it brought you to me'
From then my dewy eyes
Remained fixated on the sky
Somewhere
Something
Someone
Chose me
So gentle and free
It loved me"

FINALLY... I CAN BREATHE

"I released my burdens
To manage this grief
In that, I found another version
A breath of fresh air
She handled me with care
With her my soul was bared
She cried when I cried
Held me tight through the night
I found this strength in me
A feeling so rare
Too delicate to share
I never knew what self-love could be!"

FRAGILE PACKAGE

"Please handle with care
For my heart has shed
Too many tears to bear
And they call me strong
But all along
I flex muscle tissue
Just to reach for my angel soft
Because angels cost
At least that's what they told me
As they drifted away

It took a sunrise and sunset
To deliver the news
My warrior found his heavenly cruise
3 weeks for 4 descendants to share the
bruise
Our queen followed my warrior's cues

In these moments
I'd soon find out
My eyes would show no sign of
drought
There are many days I smile
And even then my tears are far from
mild
I'm told they help to cleanse
So I'll let my tub overflow

With these healing waters
In hopes my wings begin to grow
And I've collected feathers for show
Just so you both would know...

...I miss you dearly
I think of you frequently
I love you extremely...

Someday we'll meet again
Until then
I'll handle myself with care
Because of you
I have many more tears to bear"

MY LOVES,

"Find those parts of you that are scary and face them with love and care. After all, they are part of what makes you... you. Embrace them, take in the change, give yourself time to truly heal, and make sure you love yourself unconditionally in this process. F.Y.I The process in forever ongoing. Be kind to yourself, be gentle with your being, and be patient with your growth.

Be sure to tell yourself you love you every day, but just in case you don't hear it today or tomorrow... I love you always and forever.

Signed,

Your Favorite Feathered Traveler
Shanel Morae"

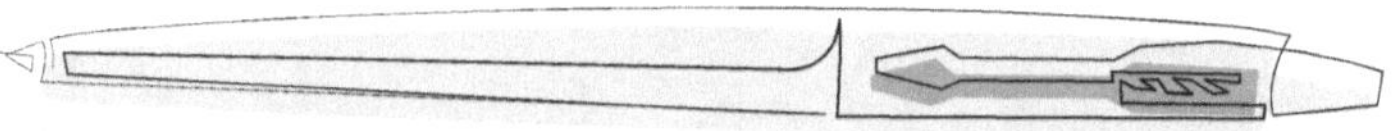

"YOUR WORDS...

"I created a section for you to write and have your own words to carry with you and look upon if you need it. I hope these pages help you as much as they've helped me!"

ABOUT THE AUTHOR

Shanel Morae is a self-published author, writer and poet. She is dedicated to finding new inspirations and new levels of freedom. "My Words... is just an extension of what she has to offer, but there are many levels to her actual written pieces of art. Her hopes are that this book along with many other poems and writings help to uplift and inspire others the way they have helped her. She encourages everyone to reflect on these words and allow them to fill your heart and soul with love and care. Her gift to everyone is her heart, her love, and the gift she was given from birth... Her Words!

"I hope you all have enjoyed "My Words... I created them especially for us! There are many more things in store, so stick around for a while because I truly have words for days.... eons even!"

- Shanel Morae

www.thefeatheredtraveler.com

The Feathered Traveler

@_featheredtraveler_

www.patreon.com/TheFeatheredTraveler

The Feathered Traveler

www.ingramcontent.com/pod-product-compliance
Lightning Source LLC
LaVergne TN
LVHW041238150826
845673LV00008B/2424

* 9 7 9 8 5 9 2 6 7 1 3 2 6 *